About the Author

I grew up in a family of nine, with two great parents. It impressed upon me the importance of being humble, of sharing, and valuing other people's feelings. I've had opportunities in my life to invent new products, build my own house, act, sing, play the violin, and write.

The Like Factor

John Martino

The Like Factor

Olympia Publishers
London

www.olympiapublishers.com
OLYMPIA PAPERBACK EDITION

Copyright © John Martino 2023

The right of John Martino to be identified as author of
this work has been asserted in accordance with sections 77 and 78 of
the Copyright, Designs and Patents Act 1988.

All Rights Reserved

No reproduction, copy or transmission of this publication
may be made without written permission.
No paragraph of this publication may be reproduced,
copied or transmitted save with the written permission of the publisher,
or in accordance with the provisions
of the Copyright Act 1956 (as amended).

Any person who commits any unauthorized act in relation to
this publication may be liable to criminal
prosecution and civil claims for damage.

A CIP catalogue record for this title is
available from the British Library.

ISBN: 978-1-80439-327-7

The information in this book has been compiled by way of general
guidance only. Neither the author nor the publisher shall be liable or
responsible for any loss or damage allegedly arising from any
information or suggestion in this book. The opinions expressed in this
book are the author's own and do not reflect the views of the publisher,
author's employer, organisation, committee or other group or
individual.

First Published in 2023

Olympia Publishers
Tallis House
2 Tallis Street
London
EC4Y 0AB

Printed in Great Britain

Contents

YOUR BEST FRIEND *Safeguarding Your Friendship* 11

BALANCING THE WHOLE PICTURE *What Is the Pulse of Your Relationship?* 17

EXPECTATIONS CAN KILL *Don't Confuse Serious Expectations with Wants and Desires. Establish a "Needs" List.* 19

BEING IN LOVE *Is "Not Being in Love" Your Biggest Fear?* 22

HOW DID WE GET TO THIS POINT? *The Evolution of Your Relationship* 25

ARGUING *Do You Argue Because You Have Nothing to Talk About?* 28

THE DARK SIDE... *Of Your Partner Is What You Will See When You Become Adversaries* 34

THE BASICS *Keep It Simple and Manageable - The Approach and the Body of Information* 37

COMPROMISE *Your Way This Time, My Way Next Time* 42

INTEREST *The Biggest Motivator of All?* 45

RAPPORT *Are You Driving a Banged-Up Jalopy That Backfires All over Town?* 48

CONFLICT RESOLUTION *How You Manage Your Conflicts Is More Important than Love and Commitment Combined for Improving the Mortality Rate of Your Relationship* 54

FRUSTRATION AND RESENTMENT *Is Your Finger on the Trigger with the Safety Off?* 57

THE PROCESS *A Grave Threat* 64

FAMILIARITY BREEDS CONTEMPT *Is This Always True?* 68

INSTANT ENEMIES *Why Is Your Partner So Often Your Opponent?* 70

THE OLD PHILOSOPHY VS. THE NEW PARADIGM *Direct Aggressive Negative Behavior Is Arsenic to Your Relationship* 72

THE GOOD THINGS WILL TAKE CARE OF THEMSELVES *Nature Intended Us to Have Relationships with Staying Power* 74

CREATING CONFLICT *Words Speak Louder than Action Where Conflict Is Concerned* 76

THE BANDWIDTH OF HUMAN RESPONSES *What Is the Difference between Direct and Indirect Behavior?* 78

BE YOUR OWN BOSS
Self-Discipline Is the Only Way 83

YOUR BEST FRIEND
Safeguarding Your Friendship

The next time you hear the expression "Love conquers all," don't believe it.

If it were true, there would never be a breakup or a divorce where both people still love each other. Yet, in reality, this is not the case. There are millions of couples that are no longer together primarily because they just can't live with each other any more. In the majority of these cases, they still truly love each other and will ache with pain after separation, but will in using their heads instead of their hearts admit that they just don't get along any more.

In the simplest of terms, they no longer like being with each other.

Now, this statement may appear far too simplistic because of all the complexities and numerous reasons surrounding the failure of a partnership, but in the final analysis, when someone walks out the door, it is largely due to their friendship falling apart.

And by examining this explanation in reverse to test its reasonability, we may ask ourselves, how often does a marriage end when both partners still like each other, when both partners are still best friends?

One must admit that the odds for success go way up when you are with someone you enjoy being around. It's human nature to gravitate to and want to spend time with someone you like. This is, of course, how all long-term relationships begin.

So, what does happen then to the multitude of great friendships year after year by the time the curtain falls at the end of the first act?

In a marriage, it is reasonable to assume that love does exist on the one hand and great affection for one another on the other, which I will term as the *Like Factor*. And most would agree that a serious relationship is not well rounded without both.

But how important is *love vs. like,* and to what extent does this relationship equation play a role in the happiness between two people?

Because love takes time to develop, time for a bond to deepen between two people requiring and involving many pleasurable and agreeable life experiences, it eventually becomes an extremely difficult thing to undo or neutralize short term. It understandably takes a significant amount of time and numerous destructive events to turn a rock-solid love into rubble.

But anyone can go from liking someone to not liking that same person in an instant. All it may take is a personal attack, an insult, hurtful words, or public ridicule for a partner to think or say, "I'm not liking you right now."

Many people might argue that "right now" only represents a small slice of time, so why make such a big deal about it? Why would I believe it critically important that you make sure this rarely ever happens, even for an instant?

Because this is the same feeling that will do you and your spouse in, in the end.

So, a clear message based on this premise may go something like this:

Say nothing that will cause your partner to "not like you" for even a moment. Do not allow them to experience this feeling for even a moment.

You see, love can take a beating. It can stand up to and survive many hits. But liking someone is a very fragile condition. One hurtful word or heated exchange has been known to ruin many a friendship or acquaintance. Measuring one's words so as not to upset a friend is an always present edit process, powerfully resident in our behavior processes. We are fully aware of it and certainly do not want to say anything that would cause a friend to "not like us."

But why are we so careful and in control with friends?

We are careful because we are concerned about the devastating results even one instance might produce. We're completely aware that even one single event could alienate a friend, or worse.

What people do not realize is that they could also lose a spouse. It just takes many more occurrences. That's all.

Now, in the beginning of a romantic relationship, we all understand and agree with this wholeheartedly. But what makes us think that with more time spent together comes invincibility? To assume this is a grave mistake.

Many of us also assume the only thing we really have to worry about is love, and how our behavior affects IT. Each of us knows very well: "what's the worry, my partner's love for me can easily handle what I'm about to say, so long as I don't cross the line."

But what about the line that has to do with *like*?

Crossing that line with a friend or acquaintance is similar to shooting a bullet their way. If it hits a vital spot it might very well be lethal. At the very least, a serious wound is inflicted. In the case of your partner however, it's probably more along the lines of throwing a small rock. Even a direct hit won't amount to much more than a few days of discomfort. But throw enough of them at one time or over the course of time and you could stone your partner to death.

Although small, frequent or constant hits such as these are big threats and big problems. They will contribute in a cumulative way toward changing a loving and affectionate relationship into a lesser version.

Allow me to pose for a moment a few of the higher-level categories responsible for divorce - loss of interest in spouse, interest in someone else, no longer loves spouse, no longer likes spouse.

Which do you think accounts for the largest number of divorces or breakups?

Let's first examine the *like factor* for the purpose of argument.

Imagine for a minute a meter was visible to only you and it measured how much you were liking your spouse at any given time, from zero to one-hundred percent. And let's apply some descriptive key thresholds. For example, because there is a direct correlation between *like* and affection, let's say that affection for your partner no longer exists at less than seventy percent. Anger begins at a lower threshold and "cold war" at another. These are all completely arbitrary, but let your feelings guide you. And at any time you looked over at it, it would tell you precisely where you stood.

Over the course of an average week, what do you think your numbers would be?

Try and ask yourself the following sobering questions. Was it ever over ninety five percent?

Was it generally over eighty percent, seventy five percent? Am I feeling affection for my partner only half the time? Do I have to admit that although I love my spouse, I hardly ever found myself liking him or her in the last seven days? Is my average an unhealthy one?

In all likelihood, you've probably never considered the importance of this measurement, but it can serve as a valuable barometer for the current climate of your relationship.

A climate or atmosphere where two people *are liking* each other a lot promotes patience and kindness and motivation to do things for, instead of against. Interest levels are highest during these periods.

When you are in the state of *not liking* your partner, you are less likely to be caring and cooperate with requests and shared responsibilities.

It may be hard to believe, but the *like factor* sets the short-term tone of your relationship. And short-term conditions that induce short-term behavior have long-term effects.

When answering the question of the importance of *love* vs. the importance of *like*, allow me to take it one step further to uncover a realization few people are aware of. Love for someone else, and I am including non-romantic relationships, will inevitably occur when anyone spends enough quality time with that person. This is why you love your partner.

This then appears to be automatic when you think about it. But to be honest, this is not what we are looking for in a marriage, are we?

What we truly want is to be "in love" with our partner.

And it is *liking* that person, not loving that person,

which plays the primary role.

That is why any variations in its levels are extremely critical to the survival of any romantic relationship.

As I mentioned earlier, many couples experience divorce and yet still love each other. It is not the breakdown or disintegration of love that causes the separation, but the ruination or depletion of *like* that does the trick.

Show me a very successful marriage, and I'll show you a couple that likes each other almost all of the time.

The connection between *like* and affection in a romantic relationship is undeniable. They are two peas in a pod. And if affection from the one you love is considered a priceless piece of the puzzle, then how much and how often that same person likes you is just as priceless.

In a marriage or serious relationship, it is not love but *like* that conquers all. Protect your partner's *like* for you. Guard it with your life.

BALANCING THE WHOLE PICTURE
What Is the Pulse of Your Relationship?

Balancing the whole picture of any relationship involves putting the positives on one side of the equation, and the negatives on the other. The positives are the accelerators of any relationship and the negatives are the brakes. The positives supply the lift, the negatives produce the drag.

When you are in balance or more preferably, when the positives outweigh the negatives, your relationship is in relative homeostasis. In the so-called "River of Life", both of you are in canoes that are at least running parallel or at best on a converging course. When the negatives outweigh the positives, a couple is on a diverging course and their relationship is in peril. The longer this goes on, the farther apart your boats get until one day, they lose sight of each other.

Reacquiring or rediscovering your partner's location now becomes difficult.

But by eliminating or reducing the negatives, the positive things that brought you both together in the first place and produced so many wonderful experiences and feelings will begin to do their work, slowly but surely. The good and healthy aspects of your relationship will soon find free sailing ahead. With less and less negative braking, the more speed a relationship can attain. Less drag results in more lift. Give your relationship a chance to literally get up into the clouds again. It was there in the beginning when *everything was positive*. It can be there again.

If you were to chart the path your relationship takes over a period of time on a line graph, and you find the ups and downs are keeping you somewhere in the middle, it invariably is the "braking effect" that is responsible. You may be averaging out between points of acceptable and unacceptable, or between fulfilling and unfulfilling, or between outstanding and mediocre. Whichever the case, if it seems that whenever a "lift" is experienced and it is soon followed by a "drag", the sum total is no gain.

❧❦

Think of where you would be if only imperceptible negative elements of behavior were present in your relationship dynamics.

EXPECTATIONS CAN KILL
Don't Confuse Serious Expectations with Wants and Desires. Establish a "Needs" List.

Expectations in a romantic relationship can kill because of what they so very often produce when they are not met, and that is disappointment and frustration, a prime breeding ground for internal conflict.

Internal conflict, or in simple terms thinking to oneself about what it is that is bothering you and what you should do about it, can create bad feelings toward your partner.

You may feel that harboring these concerns or complaints for any length of time is not healthy. So, when your internalization surfaces and you begin voicing your grievances, regardless of your approach, it quickly becomes apparent that a situation exists that requires attention and resolution. *This puts pressure on both of you.* Now you have to work on an issue or concern, or better stated, now you have to walk very carefully through a minefield together and hope you both make it out unscathed.

Expectations are synonymous with wants and desires, which may, in turn, get promoted to **needs**, a significant step in this particular chain of events, and this is where things get dangerous.

You see, if not getting what you want isn't bad enough, not getting what you think you need is even worse. This is a very important point because almost everyone views needs as far more meaningful, far more critical than wants or wishes. Almost everyone reacts with a firmer, steadfast position when it comes to his or her needs.

"I cannot compromise when it comes to what I need in a relationship or in my life. I will stand my ground and demand that these things are in place or else *this is just not working for me.*" And this is precisely where problems begin. You see, deciding what your "Need" expectations are vs. what your "Want" expectations are will determine exactly what you will not accept in a relationship and what you are willing to compromise on.

It then becomes clear that managing both these lists wisely is highly advisable due to the enormous impact the "Needs" list has on your relationship. Each need found within this list has the potential to create an unyielding, uncompromising you. Each one has the capability of creating an unhappy you, if it is not satisfied to an acceptable degree. This list is then a very dangerous one too. Manage it poorly by allowing too many items on it and you might as well place a live mine for each and every one on the road ahead of you. Neither one of you will go very far without becoming a casualty. You will find yourselves tip toeing through life when you should be running carefree down the road with few obstacles in your path.

Expectations, therefore, can also be associated with setback and injury, a razor-sharp double-edged sword.

They can either fill you or they can kill you, and have always throughout the history of human relations been a primary source of conflict and a seeding to a very large layer of *resentment* between people. A layer that may run so deep it plays a constant role in everyday living and becomes a part of the foundation of a once healthy relationship.

❦

Take a very close look at your expectations and try to separate the important ideas and images of what you feel you *need* in life with your partner from all the less critical ones that should only be found on your *wants* list.

BEING IN LOVE
Is "Not Being in Love" Your Biggest Fear?

Is "Not Being in Love" what you dread most? If the honeymoon is over, think back. Is that what was responsible for your earliest disappointments? And were these earliest disappointments responsible for the earliest tensions, frustrations, and earliest misbehavior? When you had the feeling that "things around here don't look much like there's a whole lot of love in the air any more," how did you react?

How *would* one react when one had such high hopes in the beginning, when one is in love?

You had some tremendous *expectations* when you first began. You had a vision of wonderful moments, just the right amount of romance and just the right amount of attention and devotion. You had images of your spouse coming home and sharing a lovely evening together in conversation and in each other's arms. "How was your day Honey?" And no matter if it was good or bad, you are both together now and everything is fine. Being in love meant being as one. "Our love for each other is so very strong and it shows in practically everything we do and say."

But as soon as it starts to *not show* in everything he or she does because it is *not* the same as they used to do it or say it, or it is not as often, or they have completely stopped, or now he or she is doing other things instead… a grave disappointment begins to develop. "This is not what I had in mind. I am not happy with this change in behavior at all. I know there are supposed to be ups and downs, highs and lows, but I am very upset and I do not know what to do."

This describes what happens to many young couples just starting out. They have such high hopes for a bright future with their mate. They are in love, but what they do not know is that each of their images, each of their *expectations* of what love will provide for them is quite different. And they have absolutely no idea the serious implications this simple fact conceals.

What every couple should keep in mind is that any life-long relationship moves through many different phases as time marches on. Typically, they begin with infatuation. Then a period of cooling down occurs as a couple enters into a "hitting their stride" phase. And finally, an intertwining of roots, a long-term growing and bonding together that will ultimately happen with any two people that stay together for a substantial length of time. This is where a different kind of love develops, one that enriches because it represents so much of what was built emotionally over the years. This is a deep love generated from layers of significant shared experiences.

If all of these many changes are still appealing to you, then go forward with a greater understanding that a deep love is what we all should covet first and foremost in our hearts. This is what will represent the longest period of time spent between two people during their lifetime together. Don't confuse "being in love" with true love and true happiness.

When your relationship begins to change, and it positively will, go with the flow. Real life is rarely ever anything like the expectations you cling to.

The worst thing you can possibly do is to fight this fact every step of the way with disappointment and frustration. This will cause real problems between you and your spouse. If you reject the changes, your anger will create tension, arguing and distance. If you accept the changes, you then give you and your partner the chance to move into a state of real love, deep love and true happiness. If you do not give yourselves the opportunity to move from infatuation to love, you will never make it as a successful couple.

Remember that it takes the passing of time to accomplish this.

❈

Don't reject natural change. Embrace it and realize that the highest highs in life do not come from the fast, exciting experience, but from the slow, rewarding process.

HOW DID WE GET TO THIS POINT?
The Evolution of Your Relationship

As time moves on between two people, they become more and more relaxed and invariably stray from the straight and narrow. The best foot forward that once dominated in the early going of the dating process becomes less and less prevalent in the later going of a relationship. This early positive behavior centering on concern and acceptance worked so well in maintaining a healthy rapport. But as soon as a couple becomes lazy or feels that it is not necessary to watch what they say and how they say it, this then marks the beginning of the slow erosion that will ultimately degrade anything that was once considerate, peaceful and kind.

If anyone has ever wondered why his or her relationship is nothing like the way it was in the first six months, this explanation is worthy of attention. If you've ever wondered what started the decline of incomparable treatment and impeccable manners, think back on how you spoke to one another and compare that with now. Then stop right there. You don't have to look for any other early reasons.

You spoke with care. You spoke with diplomacy. You spoke with respect for the other person's feelings. Before you even opened your mouth, you were cognizant of their feelings and how your words would affect them. Their feelings were very important to you. You handled them as carefully as you would handle nitroglycerin.

But what has happened? Somewhere along the line, things have changed, and you can't seem to put a finger on it.

The answer is that someone in your relationship decided to change the rapport.

And this process saw its beginning the first time someone uttered words that were not sensitive to the other's feelings.

Something that may have been harsh.

Something that may have been strong or aggressive or inflammatory or attacking or critical.

Something that may have put the other person on the defensive such as invasive questioning or accusations, allegations.

Someone may have expressed strong displeasure in regards to the other person's personal activities or a part of their life.

Once the first violation had occurred, the next one came easier, and so on and so on.

This slow process is the biggest and the baddest and the ugliest reason for erosion, because it is the precursor to and ground zero for almost everything that represents disharmony.

Verbal respect is the single most important aspect of a healthy rapport. Once it is violated, the enormous size of the can of worms it represents cannot be measured. It burrows and invades deeply into every aspect of a relationship.

※

We must constantly remind ourselves that we are a species that primarily communicates with one another through our mouths.

How goes speech is how the goes our relationships.

ARGUING
Do You Argue Because You Have Nothing to Talk About?

Are you controversial with your partner? Are you a devil's advocate to much of what is brought up in discussion? Do you find yourself looking across the dinner table with nothing to say and decide to go to your list of concerns or list of complaints?

If this is a dominant manner in which you discuss topics or a popular approach to cure uncomfortable silence, then to put it bluntly, you are making very poor choices when there exists such a variety of positive ways in which to communicate.

Why would you speak for the purpose of having your partner prove his or her point or to punch holes in his or her argument? And if you want to talk about something, why can't you think of anything interesting that is happening in your life or around the world, or something happy or nice or funny or pleasurable instead of going to the always-reliable default - your list of concerns, your list of complaints?

If this identifies you to any extent, then you are flirting with and most likely falling deeper into the grips of "combative interpersonal behavior." This form of relating to one another is equivalent to placing your relationship smack in the middle of a gauntlet and having both of your heads pummeled as you're running for your lives with no end in sight.

A combative style of communicating feeds on itself, getting bigger and stronger all the time, becoming a vicious circle, a vicious rapport. With more and more frequency, this pattern becomes a major part of a couple's personality. They slowly get used to it and do not realize its dysfunctional properties. It has them in the gnarls of a vice grip that squeezes so tight there's no escape. A couple caught in this dirty vortex are subjecting their relationship to target practice, to an array of slings and arrows. What may seem to be interesting banter, or the handling of important concerns is instead contributing to a hostile environment.

Using this style of communication gives rise to offensive and defensive stances, to postures of point/counterpoint, heated verbal fencing, and a potential escalation to some hard-hitting conflict. Handling problems and concerns are very important indeed, but include them as a part of your diet, not the main course.

Make sure you are providing your relationship with conversation from all the major communication groups, complete with a variety of healthy topics complimented with ample side servings of agreement, acknowledgment, positive feedback, smiling, laughter, and even nodding of the head. Your relationship is also a temple. Feed it with nourishing communication. Don't place a tourniquet around your relationship and cut off the flow of healthy conversation.

Now let's examine for a minute the popular bad habit of resorting to one of the many selections from the full assortment of "negative topics of discussion" as opposed to just sitting in silence. In simple terms, "I don't really have anything interesting, constructive, stimulating, or positive to contribute in the way of conversation, so I'll say the first thing that comes to mind, because I'd rather be talking about something than nothing at all." And many times, the easiest and simplest way to start conversation is to pick at something or someone, raise an issue of concern or doubt, complain or discuss prevailing problems, or mention a little something you're just not happy about. In short, unappealing and problematic.

The following basic fundamental is a critical category I want you to tuck away for future reference -

*Rarely say anything that will put your partner on the defensive *

The point is - just for the sake of interacting with your partner; don't take the easy way out by choosing potentially harmful approaches including criticism or complaining, or topics of issue or concern. I repeat, just for the sake of conversation. If you have an issue or concern that comes up from things you are discussing or is planned by you that you want to cover, then fine. But just because you can't think of anything to talk about, you must not enter this danger zone.

This is a bad habit. If you don't like boring and feel a need to stimulate the atmosphere, do not do it in this manner. It is much better to just sit in silence. Remember that discussing a concern or a problem can always result in a conflict, if disagreement occurs. Discretion is important here. Picking and choosing what is important enough to risk subjecting your relationship to conflict should be on your list of extreme cautions. Do not proceed indiscriminately in this area. You must try to never cause conflict through casual conversation.

And above all, do not get caught up in being the devil's advocate. Make agreeable statements. There is enough opportunity when discussing most subjects to agree on something. Try to be on the same side as often as you disagree. Remember that relationships take work. This is some of that work.

You've heard the expression, "If you didn't hear them arguing, you wouldn't hear them at all." In some extreme cases of combative communication, there are couples who know only this form of communication. The internalization goes something like this - "I want to have a conversation. Here's a sure-fire way. I'll start an argument. That'll get us talking." Now no one really says this to himself or herself, but in truth, it's a fitting description.

Personality traits and habitual behavior are scripts. Are you writing your own script or allowing someone else to? In the case of a romantic relationship, many times both individuals have a pen in hand with the capability of writing the scene "A Revolving Door" or the one titled "Constant Inappropriate Behavior." And so, they pick up their scripts and continually rehearse their parts because they just don't feel they have them quite right yet.

Ask yourself this question. Am I a negative person? Do I have a habit of concentrating much of my energies and thoughts on things that are wrong with the world, things that are wrong in my life? Do I find myself frequently or constantly wanting to fix problems no matter what their size, or having to head potential problems off at the pass, nip them in the bud, or worry about their implications?

You can "what if" yourself and your partner to death with this bad habit. This will cause more harm to your relationship than you can imagine.

Everyone has a full list of problems and complaints at their disposal for that popular game of compare and contrast with a neighbor or friend. If you think you have problems, just listen to someone else's and boy, let's look at the negativity fly.

Imagine for a moment that you and your spouse are at a party with many of your personal friends and some invited guests you are not familiar with. Try and think of some of the many ways in which people talk to each other at festive events. Typically, they make a concerted effort to be personable, maybe interesting or funny, light-hearted, fascinating, amusing or entertaining, but for the most part positive. Negativity does not abound as a popular theme at parties. People want to have a good time, and many times people will gravitate to conversations or behavior that they find interesting or fun.

This whole idea of wanting to enjoy oneself through conversation when initiating a conversation with your spouse can be therapeutic to your home life. Adopting an attitude change of this type carries with it an abundance of positive feelings on its coat tails. Rewrite your script. Make it a love story with a happy ending. This is one very good way to accomplish that.

It has been said, "People with average knowledge talk about other people. People who are well rounded talk about events. Brilliant people talk about ideas."

Become an interesting person, one who knows a little bit about everything and a lot about some things. Don't be controversial, argumentative, or a constant problem solver. Have something positive to say.

THE DARK SIDE...
Of Your Partner Is What You Will See When You Become Adversaries

If you were to ask anyone who has experienced divorce what life was like with their spouse in the last stages of marriage, there's a good chance you wouldn't hear words such as peaceful and calm. Most often it is described as extremely hostile, as couples begin to fight with more frequency and with greater intensity and greater malice. It is in fact this specific behavior that in large part becomes the final straw to break the backs of many marriages.

When two people become adversaries by consistently going outside the boundaries of calm discussion, they see and hear things that they are doing and their spouse is doing that are typical of combatants.

And a combatant is an opponent and often times an enemy to some degree, and the enemy is capable of behavior that is far from benevolent. Why then are people surprised when they see the dark side, the mean side, the hurtful side of their partner when hostile conditions exist?

Allow me to describe two sets of boundaries, one wall that people are initially aware of but quickly lose sight of, and another that they are taught by conventional wisdom not to cross over except under extreme duress.

When two people enter into a romantic relationship, they are fully aware that harsh words in the first few weeks might easily cause devastating results. This is an obvious boundary of conduct considered as the *electrified fence* in dating. It will eventually be crossed, but it's going to have to wait a little while until a suitable buffer is in place.

The investment of time builds this buffer and in so doing the couple no longer sees this wall as a stopping point. It becomes non-existent. They begin to have arguments and they begin to have fights.

They do however, manage to keep in place the second boundary for a much longer period of time, and that wall has a sign on it that reads "words that can cut deeply."

Most civilized people regard crossing this line as having serious consequences. The thinking is "I never want to say something that I can't take back" or "I don't want to say anything that might cut so deeply I will eternally regret." So, we are very mindful of this even while in the midst of serious conflict, because if we jump this barbed wire, it can get pretty ugly very fast.

"I never knew how terrible a human being he is. This is not the man I thought I married." "I can't believe how horrible she is to me. If I had only known."

When hurtful, malicious things are said to one another, statements such as these are made all the time. They are meant to describe what a partner believes he or she has uncovered, the true personality of their spouse. What they don't realize, is that this is not necessarily the case. Their partner is still a good person with good values and a good heart. They have simply been transformed into an adversary who is operating within all the acceptable rules of warfare.

Why would you expect kindness, favor, caring, or concern from your opponent? What you are witnessing can be considered normal behavior under the circumstances.

So, what has happened when it does get vicious, when the dark side is revealed?

Almost everyone has a Hyde lurking, but generally contained where friends and loved ones are concerned. What then are the mechanics behind a complete breakdown of this magnitude where a couple enters this dark world of temporary insanity and hateful behavior?

It certainly didn't just happen overnight. It takes time to evolve.

It takes small increments and instances of inappropriate tones which eventually transition to heated discussions which eventually give rise to controlled arguments that open the door to fighting and then ultimately "all-out war."

Think of it as a slow, crippling erosion that breaks down your relationship right to the brink of failure. Once a person steps across the line into the next level, they have a tendency to take that same step again. If his or her partner eventually follows, the couple is in danger of graduating on to the next and so on.

✺

If you respect the first boundary as much as you do the second and maintain it as you move through the many phases of your relationship, you are giving yourself the best chance to stay out of harm's way where hostility is concerned. If you adopt limits that neither of you cross over no matter how much anger or disappointment either experience, the dark side of the person you married will never see the light of day.

THE BASICS
Keep It Simple and Manageable - The Approach and the Body of Information

In light of the number of failed relationships in present day society, many people are of the belief that an approach of "sink or swim" when faced with the challenge of dealing with another person in a serious relationship may be a grave mistake.

So, in response to the multitude of demands and challenges found within any relationship, very often people will seek out assistance through education and instruction from any one of a variety of qualified sources.

But, in the course of their efforts, many will soon begin to discover a problematic common thread that runs through the endless supply of proposed solutions.

They eventually, more often than not, find themselves in the ongoing process of collecting and cataloging rules as they pertain to their current state of affairs so that they may be used for future ones in kind.

However, they begin to realize that the solution to today's problem is rarely ever useful for solving tomorrow's problem, or for all of next week's problems. And by the time a similar one crops up, one's memory may have difficulty providing the vivid recall needed to pluck the specifics from the appropriate personal case study. Applying the relevant catalogued approach becomes an arduous proposition.

Therefore, this common frustration experienced by so many well-intentioned, highly motivated individuals has single-handedly launched this author on a mission to develop a reasonable alternative. Because there are far too many unique situations and scenarios two people will experience in a long-term relationship, any attempt to successfully identify and categorize ground rules or instructions for each will in an unacceptable number of cases yield inadequate results.

You see, if the instructions for solving problems are as numerous as the problems themselves, then they become too convoluted and too cumbersome for practical use. How does one possibly follow them effectively, call upon the right precedent while under pressure, or for that matter ever truly know what to do? It becomes a guessing game of pin the tail on the donkey.

A common conclusion - this methodology creates a mountain of information and too much work for even the most ardent non-professional.

To solve this fundamental problem, a decidedly different approach was needed, one that would meet the challenging criteria of effectiveness and also ease of application - a set of simplistic basics.

The aim to break down something as complex and infinite as the full universe of answers to interpersonal problems into a manageable body of information was further supported by the knowledge that as workload increases, the number of people that stay the course decreases. Motivation has enemies. Most people do not come satisfactorily equipped with the level of endurance needed for most behavior modification programs. It is human nature, a reality that must be factored into any potentially successful program. Indeed, very challenging criteria.

To meet this challenge, *The Basics* presented in this book must be few and yet also thorough and comprehensive, umbrellas that offer the widest possible coverage. To fully qualify, they must also be the most significant fundamentals for this treatment.

Therefore, a core answer lies in the power and the precision of correctly chosen fundamentals. Achieving this goal would prove to be a worthy guide for the individual who is seeking uncomplicated solutions.

It is these straightforward solutions and simple techniques that I have searched for in planning this book. The results of hundreds of conversations and contributions from individuals and couples have been boiled down into a concept that would seem to be far too average and easy as to be overlooked or passed over in one glance. But, because the answers to many of life's secrets are many times the simplest, why take the long hard climb without taking a closer look?

I promise you, the ground rules found in the pages of this book will bring immediate improvements to your relationship and due to their ease of grasp and use, motivate you to stay with what will become a "new way of relating to your partner" for lasting rewards.

Allow me to now introduce the main theme in the course of these discussions.

The central focus of this book centers on the subject of *direct negative behavior*.

It is the claim of this book that a reduction of only

negative elements of verbal communication will allow a couple's many suppressed positives that are waiting in the wings to take life's stage front and center.

Eliminate the negatives from our speech and the full array of positives that are resident in each and every one of us will once again dominate the ways in which we interrelate.

The power the positives have over everyday life is enormous. They allow us to see life in Technicolor. Many are given to us through natural selection and they include such things as sexual chemistry, mating and nurturing, social pairing and emotional bonding.

These *"natural"* positive forces produce positive, appealing behavior that promotes strong ties. It is this natural form we are drawn toward and arrive at, that is of course, if nothing gets in the way. But it is our bad habits that are getting in the way, that are road blocking our natural selves. This learned, destructive behavior is what will be addressed in the following chapters.

I will attempt to convince you how some things you have come to believe as acceptable conduct are in truth some of the worst things you can do to a relationship. I will show you how to replace the many inappropriate things you do with healthier choices, which are already at your disposal because they can be found in other areas of your life, other parts of your repertoire.

The material presented in this book states that if a couple puts all of their reconstruction efforts into the health of their direct behavior, their *direct face to face style of communicating*, that this will be enough to turn their relationship in the right direction. It will allow the natural processes that brought them together in the first place and contributed to such glowing early beginnings to resurface and construct a new start.

Targeting only direct negative behavior accomplishes the second part of the primary objective, and that is keeping the program for change and the body of information modest and manageable.

Because the ultimate goal is to reach and help the largest possible audience, I have decided to keep this program within the limits of a reasonable, moderate amount of information and work that is easy to understand and easy to carry out.

The plan described in the following chapters requires a partnership to achieve modest goals and objectives, certainly within the realm of a motivated couple.

This then leaves the book's thesis and its methodology with the challenge of proving the following argument - a couple need only to address the area of "how they speak to one another" to right their ship and enjoy smooth sailing under sunnier skies.

I will break things down as I present and discuss the different types of direct negative behavior and the ways in which to manage them in an effort to lessen their destructive powers. I will help you remove the murky filter that is covering your life's lens and help you stop the vicious circle of disappointment, frustration, resentment, and contempt.

COMPROMISE
Your Way This Time, My Way Next Time

Large decisions, specifically life changing decisions, should be based on logic, not emotions. Therefore, compromise in this case is not in a couple's best interest where it defies logic. If in the process of exploring options as they relate to a big decision, sound logical recommendations abound from both parties, then any combination of choices results in a win-win situation. If however, after much debate it becomes apparent that there remains disagreement, a closer examination of cause and effect regarding the welfare of all involved must take precedent.

The outcome and its effect on the lives of the people involved must take priority over the emotional impact yielding has on one decision-maker. What makes the greatest sense for the betterment of all involved must be of paramount importance, not… what sounds the best to you because it is what you want, or "I always have to give in" or "I never get my way."

But smaller decisions and their outcomes for the most part are not as important as the emotional effect a tilted balance of power has on one or both partners.

Power imbalance affects any partnership. The meaning of partners in a relationship today is synonymous with "equal standing."

Most decisions, which are made day in and day out are generally of the less consequential variety. They can be negotiated in one of two ways - reaching a compromise or midway point, or alternating between who wins and who loses.

Each partner's emotions as they relate to winning or losing are far more important here than the end-result of a conflict - the implications the final decision has on either individual. Remember that alternating or meeting halfway with the one you love will not kill you.

The largest negative in the area of compromise is when the balance of power between two people is compromised.

It is wise to give in at times to preserve the balance of power even if you think you believe you are right. Allowing your spouse to win is more important than being right, because equality and your partner's self-worth within the relationship is ultimately more important to your happiness than getting your way.

I cannot emphasis this enough. Your partner's self-image as it relates to the balance of power in your relationship has a much greater impact on your happiness than what winning arguments or getting your way has on your happiness. Even if you believe you are a "better thinker" than your spouse holds no importance here.

Everyday decisions for the most part are not that critical. The appropriate or the wise choice has almost nothing to do with it. "Being Fair" however, has everything to do with it. If you insist on making all the decisions, then why do you have a partner at all? It sounds as if you would do just fine all by yourself. Remember, always make a genuine effort to reach a compromise or midway point, or alternate between who wins and who loses.

One very good way to realize this is to sit down and get a commitment from your partner after explaining the offered solution. In almost every single case, any fair-minded person will make the promise to live up to this kind of agreement. After all, how can anyone argue with "compromising?" How can anyone not agree to a plan that delivers a perfect fifty-fifty arrangement? And when called on the carpet, one can expect to see little or no resistance from the one who must now live up to his or her word. The key is to get the commitment up front and then to remind your partner whose turn is next.

Again, "you win this time, I win next time."

INTEREST
The Biggest Motivator of All?

The "I" word is what runs the *voluntary* world. Just as happiness is the bottom line, interest is the top line, the highest point, the chairman of the board in the hierarchy of "reasons for doing and reasons for not doing." As long as a person is physically capable and morals or ethics are not a concern, *Interest* becomes the primary answer when asking the question, "Why?"

"Why is my partner behaving the way he or she is toward me?"

The reason behind having interest or not having interest is anyone's guess. It can be something very simple or extremely convoluted. But if you've ever wondered why your partner does something voluntarily for you, it is because he or she is interested in doing so.

Sad to say the opposite is also true.

Let me emphasis these two very important points. No one has control over the level of interest within himself or herself. No one has control over the level of interest in another individual. You cannot gain interest in someone or lose interest in someone by simply trying, regardless of effort or ingenuity. Anyone who has experienced a broken heart knows this very well. It takes time to lose the high level of interest you have in a partner who has left the relationship. You can't just flip a switch.

Interest is a purely random condition and may be fueled by any number of specific or non-specific causes. In the case of almost every single romantic relationship, interest was overflowing in the early going.

Interest then is the same as "being drawn" to your lover. You are interested in being with your partner no matter what you are doing together. And your lover seems just as interested in you.

Keep in mind without interest, there is no "in love." Without interest, there is no real future.

Knowing this, shouldn't then preserving your partner's interest become first and foremost in your own best interests?

Everything you do that can be viewed as positive for the relationship can also be positive for interest preservation and growth. Conversely, everything you do that is negative, specifically direct negative behavior, can be seen for what it really is, interest injury.

If you keep attacking and angering each other, how do you think your interest for one another will fare?

You may arrive at the time and place where neither of you are interested in sharing time with the other person any more. Your interest for one another may have suffered irreparable damage.

To carry this one step further, every relationship has an emotional life span and a physical life span. The emotional, which is initially fueled and then maintained by interest, takes on a life of its own and ideally ends when the physical ends. But many couples find themselves physically together well after their emotional relationship is over. They are no longer in love. They no longer thoroughly enjoy being together or it is so few and far between. They no longer share the qualities that go hand in hand with caring, such as patience, kindness, giving, consideration, and respect.

Did one or both simply lose interest? Or, did one or both create the loss in interest?

Most likely it is the latter.

Above all things that I want you to remember, remember this - if and when you and your partner arrive at a point where a breakup is inevitable, make sure that from day one it is a result of loss of interest from reasons other than from your own hand. In other words, do *nothing* in your relationship that will author your own demise. Do nothing that will cause a direct negative impact on your partner's interest in you. It is extremely important to remind yourself that your lover's interest for you is not invincible to attack and breakdown. Do not confuse his or her love for you as something that is so strong, so immortal, so impervious to any kind of injury that you can act anyway you want. *It cannot stand up to anything you throw at it.*

Why do individuals then insist on stressing it with inappropriate behavior?

RAPPORT
Are You Driving a Banged-Up Jalopy That Backfires All over Town?

"At home, I must be able to speak in whatever tone of voice I choose. I believe it's the freedom my privacy affords me, and I believe it's what I need to effectively run my marriage."

The surprising truth is - You *cannot* afford to.

It is far too expensive. It is far... too... damaging.

Allow me to draw a reasonable parallel in an effort to shed some light on the power a good or a bad rapport has on any relationship and the impact tone of voice has on rapport. Let's do a simple, but important comparison between your home environment and your work environment. Granted, there a many differences, but a common denominator can be found in the certainty that your manner of speech can have a glaring impact on the type of response you can expect from the individual opposite you. Whether that individual is your boss or that individual is your spouse, the internal processes of either are essentially the same.

If a manager has a problem with a fellow colleague and walks into his or her office with an aggressive vocal stance or an attacking tone of voice the natural response would be shock and rejection. The other manager would immediately recognize it as extreme and inappropriate conduct. It does not conform to expected professional behavior when handling issues or concerns.

In the work place a consensus of years has set a "code of conduct", a set of rules that facilitate successful and effective communication which in turn produce a healthy environment to work in. At home, there is no established code of conduct. Almost anything goes. And as a result, it can become a "free for all", bedlam, even chaos, specifically, an unhealthy environment to live in.

The point is, as damaging as inappropriate tones are for a professional relationship, it is far more damaging in your personal life.

The reason - there are deeper feelings and emotions that exist in your marriage, such as love and attachment. You are putting these at risk.

Anyone using approaches and tones that are uncomfortable to their partner is weaving a web of ill fate and literally walking their relationship down a gang plank. This is a primary reason for what went wrong a long time ago and what will for a long time to come.

The ripples created from unsuitable advancements will eventually find their way to the shores of fear and trepidation. One partner may eventually find himself or herself walking on eggshells. This will predictably stunt the right of freedom to communicate among other things.

Another very serious common consequence is "Trench Warfare."

Defenses are constructed and offenses are readied for future engagements with the enemy. Because no one is going anywhere soon, why not dig a fox hole or build a bunker in the form of developing a thicker skin or letting it go in one ear and out the other? Either way, "I have to do something to protect myself" or "I am simply not going to let it get to me."

If you are building a defense, you are building a rift.

Eventually because it becomes apparent that you may be taking on too much damage, an offensive campaign is designed and deployed. So now both parties are waging a low-grade war because a long time ago they began to speak to one another in a fashion rarely seen in the conversations between friends or colleagues.

They decided a code of conduct was not necessary in their home and look at them now.

What once was a loving relationship is now a love-hate relationship. They both still love each other, but is it more love than hate or at times more hate than love?

The very unfortunate fact of life that I am underscoring here is this - there are multiple standards of communication that our society has set for the many types of relationships that exist in our lives. Some have explicit standards and rules as is the case in the professional realm. Some have implicit codes of conduct as in the case of friendship, and some don't have any, as found in the romantic.

Although it turns out that penalties are most immediate in the professional ranks, it is the long-term consequences that are more prevalent in your personal relationships. And that is because inappropriate speaking tones are tolerated for much longer. They are allowed to exist and in turn proliferate into the very ugly.

Let's look at some long-term repercussions, which can

be illustrated in the example of a young married couple who builds a beautiful dream house made of bricks. It looks beautiful and is very sturdy.

Imagine though, if every time you have an argument with your spouse, a brick is taken out.

I draw this parallel because every single argument or exchange of inappropriate tones comes at a cost. It chips away at the friendly, copaesthetic rapport every relationship begins with.

Every single argument you have ever had has a negative effect, be it great or small, on you and the other person involved. Arguments create negative feelings toward each other, such as anger, dislike, resentment, scorn, disdain, and in advanced stages, malice.

Feelings of love and caring are displaced and replaced. They are knocked out of the box for the time being, because in truth, most people have a hard time experiencing both love and anger simultaneously. They are mutually exclusive. They do not co-exist very well.

These are serious developments. Because although it appears to be a temporary condition, and it is at first, the more a couple argues, the closer it gets to becoming a permanent state of affairs. The positive feelings that were once responsible for a dent-free, beautiful, shiny rapport get slowly pushed aside and out of the way to make room for anger, resentment and contempt. If you allow this pattern to persist and flourish, what you wind up with is a "banged up jalopy that backfires all over town."

Being in love is a state of being everyone enjoys. When two people who are in love have a fight, how seriously does each one generally view that argument?

The seriousness of it is demonstrated whenever two

lovers make up. It feels so good for them to make up because the arguing made them feel so terrible. In a new relationship or a young marriage you might hear one person say, "Let's not fight any more. I hate fighting. Let's make love instead."

The closer you are to someone, the more in love you are with someone, the deeper the hurt. If you've reached the point where you have become more or less insensitive to a serious argument, than it may be time to take stock on the cumulative damage incurred on your relationship.

Arguments are not something to be taken lightly. Because we are complex beings with fragile emotions, the bonds that form our relationships with others are in turn fragile as well. It is their dependency on these same emotions that make them so vulnerable.

Therefore, it is my highest belief that to safeguard our feelings and the feelings of those that love us, arguing and conflict must be viewed as an extremely expensive proposition. Every time a brick is taken out, the pile of ruin gets larger, and the entire framework gets compromised. If you don't want your dream relationship to crumble, you must minimize your arguments, in frequency and in strength. Tone of voice is your most powerful weapon in the management of conflict, in the *prevention of arguments*.

When someone says, "I can't control my tone when I get upset or angry with my spouse. It's just too hard for me," I respond by saying, "Then why is it so easy when talking to your boss? Why are you so tactful then?" The plain truth is that you already do it. You already know how to control yourself. You simply just don't want to when it comes to your spouse.

It's not that you can't. You just won't!

If I were to lay a briefcase on a table filled with a million dollars and said to you, "If you can control the tone of your voice for just one week, you get the money," would you then be able to do it?

If someone followed you around with a gallon of gasoline and threatened to douse you and light you up if ever you raise your voice to your partner when frustrated, angry or upset, would you?

The point here is that in the first example you demonstrated self-control because you wanted to. And in the next example you controlled yourself because you had to.

This is undeniably true when it comes to your home environment and your work environment. At work you have to, but at home you are going to have to want to. The million dollars was a great motivator, wasn't it? But since money can't buy you love or buy you real happiness, let's take a hard look at your priorities. You would do it for money, but not for happiness, not for the sake of your relationship?

※

Controlling your tone of voice at home can be very difficult. There are no *apparent* immediate or devastating penalties. You have to remind yourself though, that the consequences are just as real. "What I am about to do is very damaging."

At home, you must be diligent and mindful in the manner you choose to speak to your spouse. Remember, it's How You Say It that matters most.

CONFLICT RESOLUTION
How You Manage Your Conflicts Is More Important than Love and Commitment Combined for Improving the Mortality Rate of Your Relationship

Just as a preservative increases the shelf life of perishable food ten-fold by preventing spoilage, becoming skilled in the handling of conflicts will act as a powerful protector that will vastly improve the life span of your relationship.

When a concern is raised by you or your partner and disagreement follows, the process of handling conflicting views is at hand. How far apart these views may be does not matter nearly as much as how you handle the conversation without thrusting yourselves into a lengthy debate or an emotional exchange.

Lengthy debates are something to be avoided or transitioned as quickly as possible into a brief, calm discussion due to the dangerous platform they reside on. They have the potential to escalate into real arguments. The longer two people go back and forth on an issue the less likely that both will maintain their cool. In most cases, it only takes one to elevate his or her tone and then a runaway chain reaction begins.

What is the best solution?

Showing sensitivity to the other's position is always

the best way to begin. One very good way to do this is by asking questions about the issue or concern in order to allow your spouse to fully explain his or her stance and feelings. This does two extremely important things. Firstly, it sends a clear signal to your partner that you are interested in his or her message and that you are truly listening. This is also reinforced due to your not responding right away with an explanation or more specifically your perspective on the topic. You are attending to your partner's first. This delays that vicious cycle of point/counterpoint, of attacking and defending long enough to potentially replace it with a constructive discussion that has a better chance of leading to a possible compromise.

An approach of this type will promote an atmosphere of cooperation when handling opposing views. Secondly, because your spouse was heard, the greater the likelihood that he or she will now listen to you more closely and be more understanding of and compassionate toward your opinion.

Debates are a form of non-cooperative interaction that can go critical and lead to a meltdown in the case of two emotionally involved individuals.

Discussions are a controlled exchange of ideas that maintain the peace and go a long way toward preserving mutual respect.

Debates are characteristic of two opposing sides going at each other's argument, with rebuttal after rebuttal. Two people who are in love have too much to lose when they subscribe to this style of handling conflict. They subject themselves to becoming habitual opponents.

Do not get into a contest of words or wills. Stay out of harm's way.

Remember, no one ever got a concussion from a discussion.

FRUSTRATION AND RESENTMENT
Is Your Finger on the Trigger with the Safety Off?

If frustration and resentment have already infected your relationship, trust me, this is no ordinary bacterial invasion that can be cured with a week's worth of antibiotics. This is much more serious. Your relationship has contracted a killer virus, an invisible predator, one that does not respond to any form of treatment. It will wreak havoc on your relationship at times and then go dormant, hiding itself, waiting for an opportunity to come out and unleash its ugly symptoms. It preys upon your conscious mind and your subconscious. It is transparent to you, the host, but does more damage than anything you can see. It fuels and escalates arguments. It is at the wheel when someone brings up things from the past while in the middle of a discussion or confrontation.

It manifests itself in the form of little or no patience, in the form of "keeping your finger on the trigger with the safety off" and all you need is a reason to squeeze.

Frustration coupled with resentment is the best target to go after when you decide to do something about your relationship. This is the area you should examine first and examine deeply to assess your problems and to resolve your woes.

Because of so severe a consequence such as drifting or breaking apart, this topic focuses on one of the most formidable destructive forces to go up against any strong and healthy relationship.

In all relationships, there are many things that require attention and serious consideration. Near the top of that list is arguably the root of so many problems, perhaps because its origin, what it owes its very existence to is so very close to your heart.

And that is *Your Expectations*.

You see, the father of frustration *is* expectations. It is why you get frustrated. And it becomes unfortunate when frustrations lie in some of the worst possible places, such as in your romantic life, more specifically, how your partner is treating you, attending to your wants, satisfying your needs. If he or she is not, then you may find yourself reacting to a reality that does not match any of your lifelong images. One that is failing, becoming less and less like the picture of what you had in mind when it came to defining your future with the one you love. The more time goes by, the fewer the similarities.

If you can honestly say, "This is not what I expected or this is not how I expected a relationship of mine to turn out."

Then you have experienced disappointments. And too many disappointments will lead to frustration. The good news is that everyone experiences some level of frustration. The bad news is that few people know how to deal with it. The critical question is how you **handle** your frustrations.

Do you respond to mounting levels of frustration with negative behavior, inappropriate behavior that upsets the apple cart, the peace and tranquility, the getting along, or do you respond with positive communication expressing your wants and needs?

If you put pressure on your partner, if you complain with heightened emotion, go on the offensive with criticism, attitude, or demonstrate passive aggressive behavior, then you are attacking like an adversary, and will eventually be treated as one.

But if you approach your spouse as a teammate, one who is trying to help the partnership, not correct it, the more probable a voluntary cooperation will ensue. Regardless of whether or not you get results, whether or not you get what you are looking for, this is the healthy choice. It is non-destructive. That is what is promoted and dissected throughout this book. Constructive, positive behavior is the only type of behavior permitted in a sound approach to ensuring a healthy, happy, long-term relationship.

I will go on to discuss ways in which to reduce and hopefully eliminate destructive and unacceptable behavior between couples. I will continually emphasis that within an adult relationship, the alternative to mature, productive communicating is not a stronger approach, not something that creates tension, not an adult's version of a child's temper tantrum. **The alternative to diplomacy is not force.**

Force will almost always be destructive when used within an equal partnership. This must not even be considered as a last resort. When all requests and suggestions and analysis and attempted compromises fail the only other choice unfortunately is leaving, moving on.

Please understand, employing destructive behavior when seeking solutions to problems will only further expand the crevasse between two people. You may be better off looking for what you really want somewhere else.

It is much better to not have what you want than to have something you don't want.

Why would you ever want to use pressure to shape someone else for the purpose of delivering your happiness? You will never get the true person. You are not allowing your partner to be himself or herself so that you can actually see what you are really getting yourself into. The other person will always eventually show his or her full wares anyway. Why not now sooner than later. Don't mask them. Do things to encourage natural behavior. Don't force a change in your partner's behavior so that your needs and wishes are being met. Instead, ask for a change and then if you get the result you were seeking, it came voluntarily. These are the ones that have a better chance to last, because they come from a wanting to on the part of your partner, not a having to.

This idea of asking instead of demanding is a whole new approach where limits are concerned, where a line in the sand is drawn between a man and a woman. These limits exist in almost every other relationship you have in your life with respect to family, friends and co-workers. Familiarity through intimacy is no excuse for behavior that crosses that line; behavior that evokes an emotional response.

Ask yourself, what right do I have to change or mold another adult human being through an uncomfortable assortment of means for the purpose of satisfying my needs? Who has the right to subject another person to pressure to conform?

No one does.

Does your partner deserve this treatment? Absolutely not. The only changes allowed in our set of rules are voluntary. And it is voluntary only if it occurs in response to a request, not a demand.

Remember, frustration must not be converted into something that can press your partner or poison your own feelings, because right around the corner from this launching pad is something even more dangerous. And that is "Resentment."

Disappointment leads to frustration which in turn can lead to resentment. This is an evolution that must never be allowed to occur in your life.

Levels of resentment are to be closely monitored. If unchecked, they can blast your relationship to kingdom come.

If you are harboring high degrees of resentment, they must be dealt with swiftly, for they are the most deadly fuses connected to the biggest bombs found in any relationship. Serious, deep-seated resentment can kill like a silent cancer that goes undetected. Before you even realize it is there, it's over. I am speaking about the type of resentment that permeates right to the core of an individual. It is the type that is always there, non-specific, almost invisible, but truly present. It is the type that is extremely difficult to shake because it was born out of anger. It is not the same as surface frustration that can more easily be rolled off one's back, put on the back burner, or forgotten about. It is not due to the fact that one partner seems to always get his or her way, or one partner's affections are all too often ignored, or one partner's ideas or wishes are being rejected. These can more easily be overlooked, forgiven, or balanced with the positives found in your relationship. These will not create an outright enemy out of your husband or wife. These will not create the type of opponent with the same degree of intensity that a fight will create. Discussions are a healthy form of communication. Arguments are not.

The point I am making is that when you get frustrated and your approach is aggressive enough to create conflict, more specifically an argument, the final result may be a full-fledged fight. This is what will do the most damage in the area of building resentment. The heat of battle between any two passionate individuals forges real weapons that puncture and cut deeply. The wounds are also very real, and if deep enough, if intense enough, one or both of you will be left with scars.

If you are carrying around scars, you are carrying around serious resentment.

Intensity, degrees, and levels are what we must emphasize and focus on when we are talking about the way in which two people interrelate. The higher the intensity, the greater the effect it has on one's emotions. And it is emotions, which pull people together and push them apart.

Frustration and resentment are time bombs that if not diffused will blow up in your face and turn your relationship into a train wreck, a heap of twisted feelings, a pile of negative emotions. They are two primary emotions that can ultimately deconstruct almost any human relationship, if the necessary degree and level of intensity is present. Authoring your own erosion is foolish. Allowing destructive forces such as these to exist and grow in your most precious possession is senseless.

※

Focus your sight on what you have grown to ignore, what you have come to accept into your home as natural, because, although it is natural for two people to argue, it is also lethal.

THE PROCESS
A Grave Threat

If and when your relationship begins to unravel, or worse, is on a course with a heading straight for the rocks, one of two forces is undoubtedly at work.

Either one or both of you is progressively losing interest in the other or the following process is applying its influence.

This five-stage process I want to introduce at this time is very common among couples and is immensely counterproductive when seeking to sustain a valued relationship.

It has a very consistent orderly characteristic and it begins with "expectations", followed then by "disappointment", "frustration", "resentment", and lastly "contempt."

These seemingly simple facts of life that we all experience are generally overlooked and overshadowed by everyday life. They are rarely paid much attention to until their levels get high enough to begin throwing red flags.

"The Process" as it's referred will be discussed and dissected in much detail in later chapters and will embrace the second theme of this book. And that is because its importance stretches across several platforms in the field of psychology beginning with **discovery**, where it will help us identify many different kinds of self-destructive behavior found in any romantic relationship. This is also where you put your arms around identified problem areas and commit to owning them. You may surprisingly find that most difficulties between you and your partner stem from one or more of the five categories.

It will also play a significant role in the **inventory** phase, where you will ultimately find where you fall on the line from good to bad relationships. In here I encourage you to measure actual levels of harmful behavior and harmful conditions.

And finally, we will utilize it in the **solutions** phase, where the objective is building specific strategies to address the problem areas.

To admit as a group that we as humans share many common traits and to identify the ones that cause us to continually shoot ourselves in the foot may allow us to enter the encouraging beginnings of discovery and the prospects of rewarding solutions.

Allow me to begin with a warning that the individual elements of this chain of events starting with "expectations" are not to be trifled with or shrugged off as non-threatening.

We've all heard the expression "familiarity breeds contempt."

Well, most of us agree that contempt is something no one would want in his or her relationship. Even at reasonably moderate levels, it can do a lot of harm to the point of being a real showstopper. Therefore, anything and everything that might lead up to it should be avoided or managed at all costs, correct?

However, if it's familiarity that causes this condition, then there is certainly nothing we can do about it. We don't want to be unfamiliar with our partner. So, what choice do we have? If it's going to happen, it's going to happen.

But what if instead, it is actually "expectations" that are responsible for contempt?

Now then that would certainly be a welcomed theory. After all, that is something we can all control if we put our minds to it.

So, the important question to answer is… how?

And since "expectations" is at the beginning of "the process" and "contempt" is at the end, is it a direct or indirect relationship and what are these intermediate steps all about? How do they contribute?

Well, let's begin your discovery here by digging into some of the missing details that are contained within and between each link in this chain to see if this connection is a stretch or if "the process" truly has a common-sense flow to it.

Here are a few high-level characteristics worth mentioning.

Each of the five stages is fully dependent upon the existence of its predecessor with the exception of "expectations" of course - it is dependent upon you, its author. And as this process moves from one step to the next, the situation and the damaging effects get progressively worse.

Each one has its own incubation period, again its dependence on the maturity of its predecessor, its own growth curve and its own degree of destructive potential.

The reality of it all is that they are very closely related, a collection of mother-daughter relationships. Once one is allowed to reach a certain maturity, the next one is born. And maturity in this reference depends upon age and frequency and sheer number of occurrences. Therefore, the existence of each phase and its specific stage of development is something we will pay very close attention to in this discussion. They are both very important in the monitoring of where you and your partner stand and in the formulation of counter measures.

※

If you keep the serious implications of these stages first and foremost in mind as you move through your daily life with emphasis on your level of "expectations", you will be placing an effective roadblock on disappointments. You will spare yourself the unpleasant frustrations and any accompanying resentment that follow. Your relationship will again be free to use the natural lift it needs to soar.

FAMILIARITY BREEDS CONTEMPT
Is This Always True?

"Familiarity breeds contempt." The last time you heard this, did you think about your own relationship and nod your head in agreement? One would think it must be correct. The expression has been around for generations with little or no opposition. Most people simply throw up their virtual hands in admission and accept it as a way of life. They believe that this is something they must learn to deal with and live with, because it eventually gets everyone. You can't control it. Like aging, there is no immunity to this malaise, no cure, no exceptions. It has a natural advantage.

Once an individual enters into a romantic relationship, time begins to take its toll, and the more time, the greater the toll. Becoming familiar with all that your partner represents, becoming close emotionally, and spending a large part of your time together appears to produce the right environment for contempt. But does is create contempt, itself?

The shocking truth is, familiarity does not breed contempt directly, but instead spawns specific *components of behavior*, which in turn produce contempt. Therefore, it is not necessarily true that it will impose its eventual, absolute control, causing a similar fate shared by so many.

The answer can be found in these common

components of behavior. And it is these components that we will examine, break down, and offer explicit direction on how to manage. You will find that you are actually in control of this phenomenon, if you take charge of the intermediate behavior that produces the all too familiar end result. Familiarity by itself is not the culprit. It is only the catalyst. The main ingredients are universal, learned and stored behavioral patterns that most of us eventually call to action. And once called, the effects become too enormous and far reaching to control. Pandora's box has been opened and the beautiful rapport once enjoyed between two people has been changed forever.

INSTANT ENEMIES
Why Is Your Partner So Often Your Opponent?

Typically, in close relationships, the fastest way to create a serious opponent out of a loving partner is not through content, but through tone of voice.

To best illustrate this point, let's take a look at how an aggressive tone of voice affects two people who are not in a relationship.

Road rage is a perfect example of the profound effect explicit verbal aggression has when directed at another human being. The *"fight or flight"* response is activated. Although this is more an extreme case situation than what most domestic confrontations fall under, the physiological and psychological responses are the same, only the degree is different.

When a stranger verbally assaults another stranger, the possibility that the recipient will become angered or frightened is nearly one hundred percent. The likelihood that they will enter into an intelligent, well thought out discussion is close to zero. The initial physiological responses experienced by both individuals all but completely prohibit productive interaction. The most common result is *"instant enemies."* Even the act of raising one's voice at another person can result in the *"fight switch"* being thrown. This approach if used when attempting to accomplish anything positive by the initiator accomplishes just the opposite. It creates non-compliance. It creates non-cooperation.

If an inappropriate tone of voice is this lethal between strangers, and typically is very damaging for most types of relationships, then why is it so widely accepted or more precisely tolerated in a marriage? Is it because a constant close proximity creates tensions and hostilities that would not normally be present? Is it because of the tiring effects constant disagreements and minor conflicts have on two people on a frequent basis? Is it because everyone else does it? Does this make it unavoidable?

❧

If one is looking to maintain a friendship, maintain a harmonious relationship, maintain good terms, then an appropriate tone of voice is a necessity. What you say to another human being is immensely less important than "How You Say It."

THE OLD PHILOSOPHY VS. THE NEW PARADIGM
Direct Aggressive Negative Behavior Is Arsenic to Your Relationship

One of the main purposes of this book is to create a new philosophy for the reader, a completely new paradigm composed of new beliefs and new attitudes. I boldly require that at minimum, some part of this new framework be incorporated into your attitude profile. A complete adoption would mean a complete transformation. But the more you repeat these *"principals to live by"* to yourself and practice them as you practice self-control, the more effective the removal of negative behavior will be from your life.

My intent is to firmly replace old, long-standing ideas that are a root of failure in any relationship with brand new beliefs. I promise you, although they may appear difficult to adopt and apply when under pressure, they will bring about a peace and a calm that will one day move you. Conversely, as you don't know how you got to where you are now, you will notice a marked course change in your relationship as time passes. Where a conflict may have previously caused one or both of you to get upset, snuffing out potential hours of enjoyable time together, a new way of relating will now promote smooth sailing. Remember that what you see in the left-hand column is *not* working.

Old Philosophy	New Philosophy
If two people love each other, they'll fight.	If two people love each other, they'll show extraordinary patience.
Arguing is just a fact of life you must accept, so why try to resist it.	Arguing is to be avoided or managed at all costs.
I am allowed to get irritable toward my partner when I am stressed out. He or she should understand	I am absolutely not allowed to use my partner as a target or dumping ground.
When my partner does something stupid, I am justified in climbing all over him or her.	I will not go beyond a stern tone confined to no more than stating displeasure or disappointment, expressions of anger are prohibited here.
I expect a certain level of behavior and if I don't get it I am allowed to express anger and apply pressure.	I am no longer allowed to apply pressure based on my wants or expectations; only in cases where my partner is not living up to prior agreements.
I have a right to place demands on my partner if I believe I am right in doing so	No one has the right to tell another adult what to do. I can only request or suggest.

THE GOOD THINGS WILL TAKE CARE OF THEMSELVES
Nature Intended Us to Have Relationships with Staying Power

Eliminate direct negative behavior toward your partner and the positive elements that are present in every person, including you and your spouse, would soon dominate and profoundly affect your relationship.

Let's get back to the positives I mentioned earlier when discussing your relationship balance scale. Everyone comes fully equipped with more than enough mental and physical characteristics to enter into and develop a healthy and exciting relationship. These are pro relationship qualities and attributes that stir up the many positive feelings and emotions experienced between a man and a woman. They are given to us by nature, by our genes, and their purpose is to bring and keep us together for a very long time.

Combine attraction to the opposite sex with long term bonding forces, transparent but real, and there exists a powerful drive that shapes our very lives.

We as humans were meant to have relationships with staying power. Our offspring are dependent upon both parents until well after puberty for food, protection, instruction, and psychological development. The survival of any species' young is directly related to their ability to eventually function and provide for their own needs. Our children's inability to do this for many years requires the parents stay together as a unit for nearly two decades.

What steps did nature take to ensure this?

Firstly, the instinct to bond is aided by the pleasure we receive through our sense of touch. Our species is one of the very few that engages in sexual activity for the sake of pleasure and pleasure alone. The female does not have to be in heat to excite the male sex drive. Human beings are also one of the very few mammals with little or no body hair. Nerve endings located in the skin are activated much easier with no fur or hair covering and in turn stimulate our large pleasure center in our very large brains. This promotes re-engaging in the stimulating activities that are partly responsible for both bonding and emotional attachment. Since our emotions are directly connected to our senses, physical intimacy has a profound effect on the development of feelings. Depending on the individual this can be overwhelming.

"Falling in love" in many cases, is synonymous with both a mental and physical bonding, however, it is the physical realm where nature flexes its genetic muscle. Physical intimacy and pleasure, therefore, is one of nature's most powerful means to bring together and keep together a man and a woman for a substantial length of time.

A lifetime.

CREATING CONFLICT
Words Speak Louder than Action Where Conflict Is Concerned

Let's take a close look at a few behavioral patterns you may have noticed between members of one typical family found almost anywhere in America today. As you read this, decide for yourself if you belong to this group or if you can picture a potential future such as this one.

Allow me to begin by asking you why a vast majority of parents have a higher level of patience, understanding, and compassion for their children than for their spouse? Why are they more careful with how they speak to their children, how they handle conflicts, and in general how they nurture that relationship more so than their marriage? Is it because the children are subconsciously viewed as innocent of personal affronts and transgressions to the parent, where the spouse is not? Is it a case of unconditional love for their children vs. conditional love for their spouse? Do parents feel that their children need them for much more than their spouse needs them?

Most agree that the bond between a parent and a child is much stronger and is more impervious to damage than the bond between a husband and a wife. A lifetime of love, understanding, and staying connected is virtually guaranteed between a parent and a child, but not so for spouses. Now you wouldn't expect this to be true, taking into consideration that the same level of love and commitment *should* exist in a marriage as it does in a parent child relationship. Why then do we not treat all members of the family equally in terms of tone, approach, and patience? We love all of them equally. Why then doesn't your spouse deserve the same considerations and treatment? If love and commitment is the same in both sets of relationships, what is the cause behind the differences in behavior?

The things responsible are the buildup of frustrations and the existence of hidden resentment and contempt.

But if one answers with the claim that familiarity and close proximity breeds contempt, then why is it so pronounced between a husband and wife and rare between a child and a parent, when they all share the same house?

If we can identify some of the reasons why a spouse will approach a spouse differently than they approach one of their children, then maybe we can get at the root of this dysfunction.

THE BANDWIDTH OF HUMAN RESPONSES
What Is the Difference between Direct and Indirect Behavior?

Once you grasp this fundamental concept and put it into practice, you will successfully remove a vast amount of destructive negative behavior and a large part of any strong negative feelings that may exist from your relationship. The following discussion addresses a large sector and source of erroneous deductive reasoning whose products are frustration and anger. Removing this sector from your life will cut the battle in half, leaving only "direct behavior" as the central core of our remaining discussions.

The following statement is meant to help you understand an upcoming fundamental principal that addresses this section - *Unintentional and indirect are one and the same.*

Now, we are familiar with how to treat something that is unintentional, correct? The individual is dealt with from a position of complete understanding that includes both patience and pardon. He or she didn't really mean it. It was unintentional. How can you get mad at that? You might ask them to be more careful next time, or express disappointment, or suggest a more desirable behavior. But striking out at them is a bit too harsh, because after all, how can you hold someone responsible for something that they did not mean to do? Now comes the hard part. From now on, we will treat indirect behavior the same way we treat an unintentional act.

Indirect behavior is defined as actions or speech on the part of your partner that is NOT directed at you. Direct behavior is therefore the opposite.

Indirect behavior is something a person is always allowed to do, with one exception, and that is if it goes against a prior agreement, arrangement, or promise. It is their life and they can run it any way they choose. There is no need for a person to feel responsible in any way to another if he or she is simply going about his or her own business.

The following basic fundamental is a critical category we want you to tuck away for future reference -

** Never Hold Your Partner Immediately Responsible for Indirect Behavior **

This means that if your partner is doing and saying things that are not directed *at you and are not about you*, then he or she is temporarily absolved of any effect it has on you. If what your partner does or says in this case affects you in any way whatsoever, it is to be treated as unintentional on the part of your partner, therefore, your partner is to be completely excused by you for the moment. He or she didn't mean to upset you, again, so how can you hold them responsible? Most of the time your partner won't even know that what has been done or said *has* affected you. To reiterate, it was unintentional. All indirect activity and behavior is to be treated as purely unintentional until you question his or her motives or reasons. You must gather information if you feel it is necessary to draw a conclusion one way or the other as it applies to intent. In the meantime, complete innocence prevails until proven guilty of intentional conduct.

Never translate the meaning of indirect behavior or activities - why someone is saying or doing something - without asking questions to find out for sure whether *intent to hurt exists or not*, no matter how obvious something appears.

*Translating is the same as guessing - Never Guess! *

Guessing is one of the most dangerous games you can play. It can result in the *invalidation* of your partner, which carries extreme, injurious consequences. Erroneous deductive reasoning is a critical mistake that will often cause inordinate amounts of unnecessary grief. It is so often erroneous because the odds of guessing correctly are extremely low. There may be hundreds of reasons anyone can think of why someone does something, but there is only one that fits. And the only one who knows is the person who did it. So, don't bother guessing, because you will never get it right. Ask instead.

Now, getting back to intent. If there was intent to do harm, and this is very rarely the case, then there is responsibility, and your partner must now face the charges and the punishment.

Even if you feel there was an infraction against your person - what you believe to be inappropriate behavior or conduct, but there is no intent, then you must handle the situation with care. Your approach must not include emotional elements. You must confine yourself to only explaining your feelings and discuss how his or her behavior has affected you, nothing more. There must be no display of emotion, no anger, no assault, no reprimand.

Remember that it is to be treated the same as any unintentional act. You might ask them to be more careful next time, or express disappointment, or suggest a more desirable behavior.

Don't show your partner your feelings. Inform your partner of your feelings.

You may tell him or her how upset you are or how angry he or she made you feel. But no attack or retaliation in any form is permitted. Specifically, what is being accomplished here is you are letting your partner know that you are acknowledging the fact that he or she is unaware that what was said or done had indeed bothered you. You are not holding them responsible, therefore, the reason for no display of anger.

It is extremely important to understand the following - *whatever emotions you are feeling will have to be managed by you until you can speak with your partner.*

In other words, you must conceal any anger or disappointment from your partner until you can discuss the problem. The reason - don't affect the present with something you may be wrong about or your partner is unaware of. Try with all your will to put your feelings aside for the time being until you can confront your loved one.

Why ruin the present when a simple question by you followed by an acceptable answer from your partner might just diffuse your internal situation.

What then follows would be coming to terms with the

problem if it still exists, and hopefully getting cooperation from your partner that he or she will try not to do it again.

Remember that you have more control over your direct behavior and how it affects your partner than indirect behavior that is translated by your partner. Pay close attention to what you can control and allow yourself to incorporate more flexibility in the form of waiting to discuss your partner's actions when the time is right.

This entire approach for dealing with your partner's indirect behavior will bulletproof your relationship to erroneous interpretations, premature reactions, and unnecessary tensions. It will help prevent you from falling into these common traps. By managing your negative emotions, you are managing your number of arguments. And that is what we are here to do - learn how to keep the apple cart upright - learn how to minimize the potential for clashing and lashing out at each other. Remember, every argument is expensive. Every argument comes at a cost.

BE YOUR OWN BOSS
Self-Discipline Is the Only Way

When you took your job, you knew appropriate verbal conduct went along with the territory. When you got married you didn't.

In the professional world, the damage may be irreparable, with reduced chance for promotion or worse, loss of employment. In your personal life damage may translate into an unfulfilled relationship or worse, divorce. The message is, you simply cannot afford to behave this way in either facet of your life. It is far too expensive.

An inappropriate tone of voice over time can cost you your job or cost you your marriage. Which is more important to you, your job or your marriage? Why then do you take extra measures to prevent it from creeping into your professional relationships? You are much too careful, even in the event that you might become angry. Yet, at home, who cares? "My partner will just have to accept me for the way I am."

Well, eventually, your partner will not. He or she will reject you and all you stand for. You become opponents instead of lovers. You become combatants and roommates instead of friends and spouses.

To achieve a more pleasing tone of voice in your significant relationship at home requires discipline. *Become your own boss.*

Some employees when unsupervised for long periods of time become non-productive and less disciplined. No one is watching, so they slack off. When a time clock is used, most employees are less likely to be late for work. Salesmen in the field are on the honor system to apply themselves at least eight hours a day, five days a week. But do they? When you take a close look and discover the number of people that become lazy, simply don't put the effort out when they are not forced to, it can be very alarming. When people are put in a situation where there is no supervision, and it is up to them to be their own boss, many of them would be fired if a hidden camera were present. But many would not.

In your home there is no supervision governing your behavior. If a psychologist were present all the time, whose expressed purpose was to document inappropriate behavior, how do you think you would behave? You would probably walk the same straight line you walk at work with your superiors.

The fact is there is no one to monitor you in your personal relationship but yourself. You can allow yourself to become lazy, but you can not afford to. If you decide to be your own boss, be a good one. Become that individual who is always diligent, who does not slack off, who is always on time, who does not need supervision. There is no hidden camera in your private life. There is only self-discipline.